Maths
made easy

Key Stage 1
Ages 6-7
Advanced

Author Sue Phillips and Linda Ruggieri
Consultant Sean McArdle

Certificate

Congratulations to ....
for successfully finishing this book.

(write your name here)

 You're a star!

Up to 100

Write the missing numbers on the kites in each row.

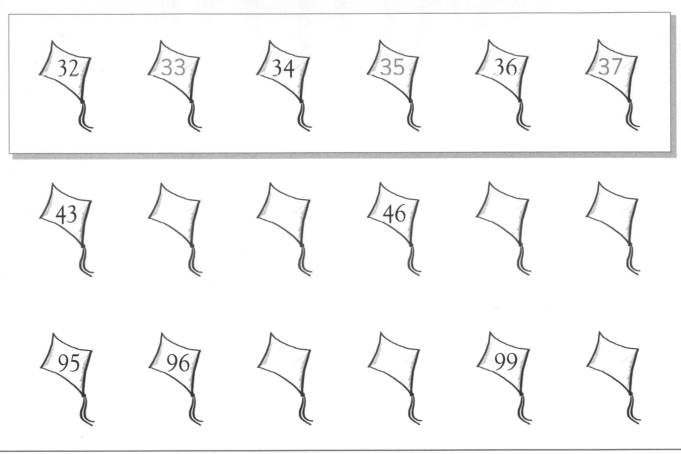

Fill in the missing number words in each row
by choosing them from the box.

Thirty		Twenty		Forty		Seventy
	Twenty-six		One hundred		Twenty-nine	

Ten	....	Thirty	....	Fifty
Sixty	....	Eighty	Ninety	....
Twenty-five	....	Twenty-seven	Twenty-eight	....

Read the words. Write the correct number.

Eighty-five ☐   Ninety-nine ☐   Fifty-six ☐

Changing tens

Write the number and then the word in each row.

	Number	Word
The value of 4 in 47 is	40	Forty
The value of 8 in 183 is		
The value of 6 in 62 is		
The value of 2 in 126 is		
The value of 5 in 150 is		

Write the answer as a number and as a word in each row.

	Number	Word
If you change 21 to 51, how much value did you add?	30	Thirty
If you change 43 to 83, how much value did you add?		
If you change 65 to 35, how much value did you subtract?		

Circle the numbers in which the 2 has a value of 20.

| 82 | 28 | 125 |

Fact families

Complete the facts for each family.

3 + 5 = ☐ 8   5 + 3 = ☐ 8   8 − 3 = ☐ 5   8 − 5 = ☐ 3

2 + 7 = ☐   7 + 2 = ☐   9 − 2 = ☐   9 - 7 = ☐

3 + 4 = ☐   4 + 3 = ☐   7 − 3 = ☐   7 − 4 = ☐

4 + 5 = ☐   5 + 4 = ☐   9 − 4 = ☐   9 − 5 = ☐

1 + 6 = ☐   6 + 1 = ☐   7 − 1 = ☐   7 − 6 = ☐

6 + 4 = ☐   4 + 6 = ☐   10 − 4 = ☐   10 − 6 = ☐

5 + 2 = ☐   2 + 5 = ☐   7 − 5 = ☐   7 − 2 = ☐

1 + 8 = ☐   8 + 1 = ☐   9 − 8 = ☐   9 − 1 = ☐

7 + 3 = ☐   3 + 7 = ☐   10 − 7 = ☐   10 − 3 = ☐

Write the facts for the fact family 3, 6, and 9.

☐ + ☐ = ☐   ☐ − ☐ = ☐

☐ + ☐ = ☐   ☐ − ☐ = ☐

Quick adding

Write the answers.

7 + 2 **9**	9 + 0	2 + 3	5 + 4	4 + 6
1 + 2	10 + 0	4 + 4	5 + 3	4 + 2
5 + 2	6 + 3	3 + 3	5 + 0	9 + 1

Write the missing number.

$4 + 6 = 10$ $2 + \boxed{} = 8$ $6 + \boxed{} = 9$

$\boxed{} + 1 = 8$ $\boxed{} + 5 = 7$ $3 + \boxed{} = 7$

$0 + \boxed{} = 10$ $4 + \boxed{} = 6$ $\boxed{} + 4 = 8$

Write the number sentence to match the pictures.

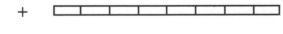

$\boxed{} + \boxed{} = \boxed{}$

$\boxed{} + \boxed{} = \boxed{}$

Adding two-digit numbers

Use the number lines to answer the equations in each row.

13 14 15 16 17 18 19 20 21 22 23 24 25 26 27 28 29 30 31 32

13	14	21	17	11
+ 12	+ 13	+ 11	+ 10	+ 21
25				

20 21 22 23 24 25 26 27 28 29 30 31 32 33 34 35 36

24	21	23	25	20
+ 12	+ 11	+ 10	+ 10	+ 13

28 29 30 31 32 33 34 35 36 37 38 39 40 41 42

30	28	31	30	29
+ 12	+ 10	+ 11	+ 10	+ 10

Use the counting blocks to solve the equations.

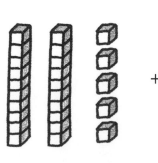 + 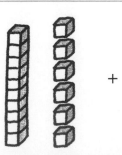   25 + 10 = ☐

   16 + 12 = ☐

Adding numbers vertically

Add the ones, then add the tens in each equation.
Write the answer.

Add the ones,	then the tens.	Regroup and add.
Tens Ones	Tens Ones		
7 4	7 4	6 2
+ 1 2	+ 1 2	+ 1 9
8 6	**8** 6	**8** 1

63	45	14	35	54
+ 31	+ 20	+ 14	+ 31	+ 22

75	18	14	74	50
+ 23	+ 20	+ 82	+ 11	+ 32

Add the ones, and regroup your answer as tens and ones.
Then add the tens to solve each equation.

5 3	4 8	1 6	6 2	4 4
+ 3 8	+ 3 2	+ 1 4	+ 1 9	+ 4 7
9 1				

5 5	3 9	2 8	4 6	1 7
+ 1 8	+ 3 3	+ 1 4	+ 2 9	+ 4 6

Write the answer to each equation. Shade the shapes where
the answer is 79.

3 7	5 2	33	6 1	43	2 4
+ 4 2	+ 2 7	+ 59	+ 1 8	+ 15	+ 5 5

Problem solving (addition)

Read each story. Then write the equation and solve the problem.

Mr. Lopez sells apples. He has 4 baskets of 10 apples, and another
8 loose apples. How many apples does he have in his store?

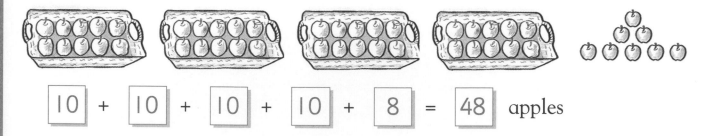

10 + 10 + 10 + 10 + 8 = 48 apples

Mum is making apple pies. She has a basket of 10 apples.
She buys another basket of 10 apples and another 3 single apples.
How many apples does she have now?

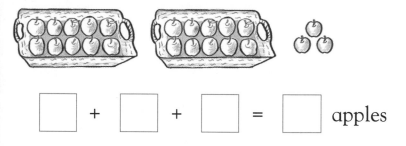

☐ + ☐ + ☐ = ☐ apples

Paul is selling muffins at the school bake sale. He sells 24 muffins in the
morning and 21 in the afternoon. How many muffins did he sell in all?

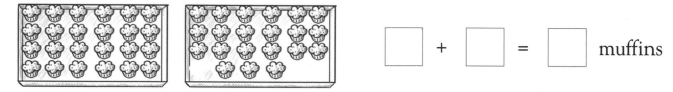

☐ + ☐ = ☐ muffins

Write the answer. Then draw pictures of objects to match
the number sentence.

11 + 12 = ☐

Subtraction action

Write the answers to these subtraction problems.

10	9	7	10	8
− 7	− 3	− 5	− 2	− 4
3				

9	5	6	9	4
− 6	− 3	− 1	− 4	− 4

3	7	6	10	2
− 1	− 2	− 3	− 5	− 2

Fill in the missing number in each subtraction problem.

8 − 6 = 2   ☐ − 7 = 1   ☐ − 2 = 2

☐ − 6 = 4   ☐ − 7 = 2   ☐ − 8 = 2

Complete the number sentences. Shade in the animal that
has a number sentence with an answer less than 5.

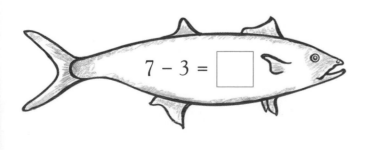

7 − 3 = ☐

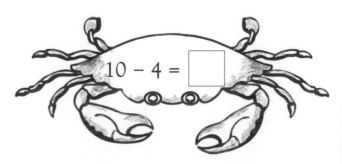

10 − 4 = ☐

Find the difference

Count backward on the number lines to solve the equations in each row.

24 25 26 27 28 29 30 31 32 33 34 35 36 37 38 39 40 41 42

42	35	39	37	41
− 11	− 10	− 15	− 11	− 10
31				

65 66 67 68 69 70 71 72 73 74 75 76 77 78 79 80 81 82 83 84 85

80	85	75	76	83
− 10	− 13	− 10	− 11	− 12

50 51 52 53 54 55 56 57 58 59 60 61 62 63 64 65 66 67 68 69 70

70	62	65	65	64
− 20	− 12	− 10	− 11	− 12

Draw dots in the boxes to show 22 − 12 = 10.

What's the difference?

Find the difference in each subtraction problem.

Subtract the ones,	then the tens.	Regroup and subtract.
Tens Ones	Tens Ones	4 13
7 4	7 4	5̶ 3̶
− 1 2	− 1 2	− 1 4
6 **2**	6 2	**3 9**

48	45	88	54	86
− 30	− 15	− 77	− 33	− 54

89	34	52	74	96
− 54	− 13	− 31	− 23	− 35

Find the difference by regrouping. Add 10 more to the ones.
Make the tens less by 1. Subtract the ones and then the tens.

6 12				
7̶ 2̶	8 7	5 3	6 5	8 4
− 5 4	− 2 9	− 2 6	− 4 7	− 6 7
1 8				

5 5	3 6	7 5	4 4	6 5
− 1 6	− 1 7	− 4 6	− 2 7	− 4 9

Draw balloons to show this subtraction
sentence. Then write the answer.

17 − 12 = ☐

☆ Problem solving (subtraction)

Read each story. Solve the problem.

Amy has 65 pages to read for homework. She has already read 31 pages. How many pages does she have left to read?

$\boxed{65}$ − $\boxed{31}$ = $\boxed{34}$ pages

It is 32 miles to the airport. Mr. Miller has already driven 21 miles. How many more miles does Mr. Miller need to drive to get to the airport?

$\boxed{}$ − $\boxed{}$ = $\boxed{}$ miles

Juan has a list of 21 items to buy at the store. He has already found 11 of the items. How many more items must he find?

$\boxed{}$ − $\boxed{}$ = $\boxed{}$ items

Find these words hidden in the puzzle. Go across or down.

takeaway	difference
subtract	minus	equal

C	Y	M	I	O	S	T	J	H	S
T	W	V	F	P	U	L	K	Z	T
U	A	O	E	G	B	D	X	S	A
H	M	A	S	V	T	Y	I	U	K
D	I	F	F	E	R	E	N	C	E
R	N	E	S	Q	A	D	G	O	A
K	U	L	Q	U	C	X	C	B	W
T	S	I	O	A	T	K	Q	D	A
E	R	P	K	L	I	V	F	J	Y
W	U	H	S	Y	E	P	L	A	X

Bigger or smaller?

Draw the crocodiles.
They always eat the bigger numbers!

16 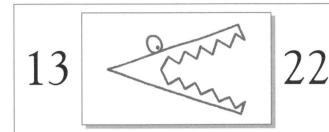 14   13 22

25   30   33   43

38   43   26   46

55   39   65   80

50   42   71   72

80   70   91   90

Ordering

Find the totals.

£2.20

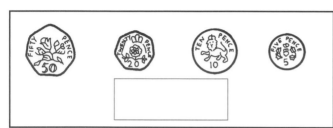

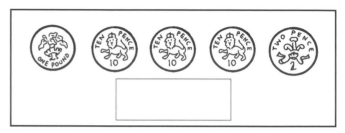

Write the totals in order, largest first.

1st £2.20   2nd   3rd   4th   5th

Find the totals.

92p

Write the totals in order, smallest first.

1st   2nd 92p   3rd   4th   5th

Shopping

Write the total amount spent. Draw the coins you will need.

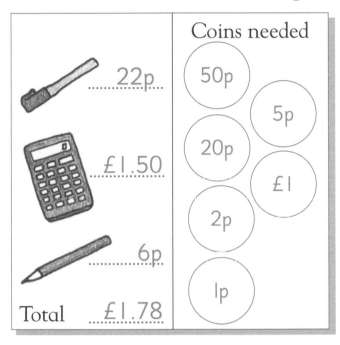

	Coins needed
	50p
22p	5p
	20p
£1.50	£1
	2p
6p	
	1p
Total £1.78	

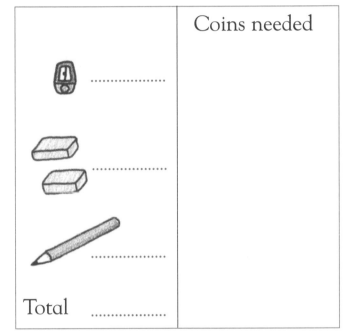

Coins needed

....

....

....

Total ....

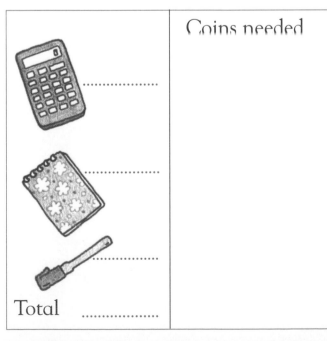

Coins needed

....

....

....

Total ....

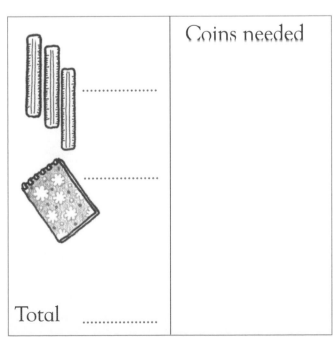

Coins needed

....

....

....

Total ....

2x table

Draw the pictures. Write the number sentences.

Sasha has 4 hutches. There are 2 rabbits in each hutch.

4 x 2 = 8 rabbits

Joel has 3 pockets. There are 2 pens in each pocket.

Mrs Reaves has 6 flower pots. There are 2 flowers in each pot.

Mr Hastings has 5 fish. Each fish has 2 eyes.

Share them out equally. Draw the pictures, then write the number sentences.

There are 16 birds. There are 2 trees.

There are 18 noses. There are 2 monsters.

10x table

Find the right label for each balloon.
Only use the labels you really need.

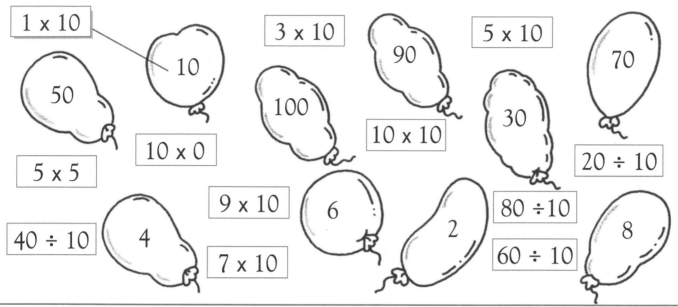

1 x 10 | 3 x 10 | 5 x 10

50 | 10 | 90 | 70

100 | 10 x 10 | 30

10 x 0 | 20 ÷ 10

5 x 5 | 9 x 10 | 6 | 80 ÷ 10 | 8

40 ÷ 10 | 4 | 2

7 x 10 | 60 ÷ 10

Use the 10x table to solve these problems with x or ÷.

You buy 5 books at 10p each. How much do they cost altogether?

$$5 \times 10 = 50p$$

If you had 90p and you gave an equal amount to your 10 friends, how much would they have each?

$$90 \div 10 = 9p$$

If there were 20 cakes and 10 children, how many cakes would they have each?

4 mice had 10 babies each. How many baby mice were there altogether?

There were 70 flowers and 10 pots. How many flowers were in each pot?

You have £1.00. Have you got enough to buy 9 pencils at 10p each?

You have 30 sweets in a bag and you give them all to your 3 friends. How many sweets can you give each of them?

5x table

Find the right pot for each flower. Not all pots will have a flower.

Use the 5x table to solve these problems with x or ÷.

If there were 20 balloons and 5 children, how many balloons would they have each?

> 20 ÷ 5 = 4
> balloons

Buy 8 peaches at 5p each. How much will they cost?

> 8 x 5 = 40p

The teacher had 35 stickers and 7 hard-working children. How many stickers could they each have?

4 squirrels had 5 acorns each. How many acorns did they have altogether?

There were 30 crates shared between 5 lorries. How many crates were on each lorry?

Buy 7 stickers at 5p each. How much will they cost?

A woman has 50p. Does she have enough money to buy 9 plums at 5p each?

Rectangular arrays

Count the rows and columns. Then write the multiplication sentence.

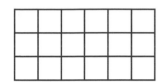 | 2 | rows and | 4 | columns | 2 x 4 = 8 |

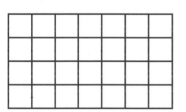 [ ] rows and [ ] columns [_____]

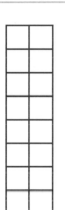 [ ] rows and [ ] columns [_____]

[grid] [ ] rows and [ ] columns [_____]

Connect the words on the left with the matching picture on the right.

3 rows and 7 columns

1 row and 10 columns

2 rows and 4 columns

Real-life problems

Look at the picture. Answer the questions.

What time is it? ....

Today is Friday. What day was it yesterday? ....

How many cakes can each person have? ....

If half of the apples were eaten, how many would be left? ....

If each person had 2 drinks, how many drinks would there be altogether? ....

How many more sandwiches are there than apples? ....

If 13 sweets were eaten, how many would be left? ....

Each parcel contains 2 presents. How many presents are there altogether? ....

What shape are the sandwiches? ....

Is there an odd or an even number of chairs? ....

Estimating mass

Circle the animal that is probably heavier in each pair.

Circle the animal that is probably lighter in each pair.

 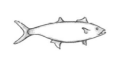　　　

Circle the correct ending to each story.

Jack and John went to the farmers' market. Jack bought a bag of apples. John bought a bag of string beans. Both bags were the same size. The bag of apples probably weighed:

more than the bag of string beans　　　　about the same as the bag
　　　　　　　　　　　　　　　　　　　　of string beans

less than the bag of string beans

Ally and Laura carried books to the library. They each had five large books. Laura's books probably weighed:

more than Ally's books　　　　　　less than Ally's books

about the same as Ally's books

Measuring lengths

How many centimetres long are these objects?

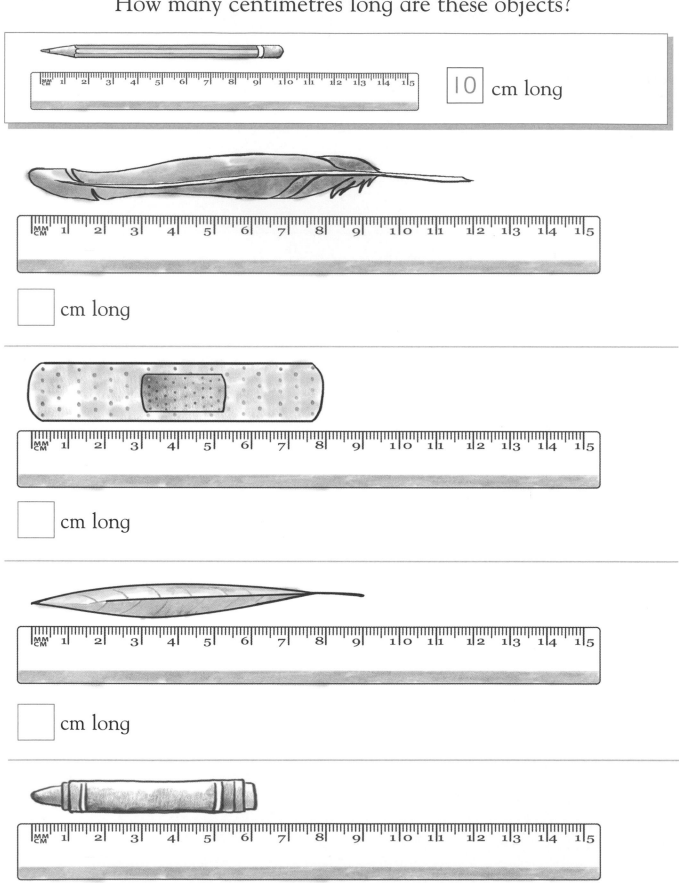

$\boxed{10}$ cm long

$\boxed{}$ cm long

$\boxed{}$ cm long

$\boxed{}$ cm long

$\boxed{}$ cm long

Problem solving (lengths)

Read each story. Then add or subtract the lengths
to solve the problems.

Tom and Jason measured the flowers they found. Tom's flower measured
25 cm while Jason's was 20 cm long. What was the difference in the
lengths of the flowers?

25 cm – 20 cm = 5 cm

Jess bought a piece of ribbon that was 27 cm long. Mary bought one
that was 15 cm long. How long were the two pieces altogether?

[ ] cm + [ ] cm = [ ] cm

Maria's coloured pencil was 22 cm long. Juan's coloured pencil was
15 cm long. How much longer was Maria's pencil than Juan's?

[ ] cm – [ ] cm = [ ] cm

Maya watched an ant crawl 7 cm Then the ant crawled 17 cm more.
How many centimetres did the ant crawl altogether?

[ ] cm + [ ] cm = [ ] cm

Linda's drawing paper was 30 cm long. Sue's paper was 25 cm long.
How much longer was Linda's paper than Sue's?

[ ] cm – [ ] cm = [ ] cm

Anita has a piece of string that is 24 cm long.
Can she make two equal pieces from this piece of string?   Yes   No

How long would each piece be? [ ] cm

Telling the time

Draw the hands on the clock
to show twenty past **5**.

Draw the hands on each clock to show the time.

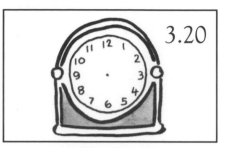 3.20

 5.30

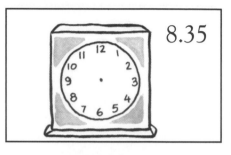 8.35

 7.45

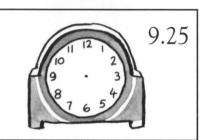 9.25

 11.15

Write the time shown on each clock.

Differences between times

Look at the time on the first clock in each row. Then look at the time on the second clock. What is the difference in time between the clocks? Circle the correct answer.

    1 hour   half hour   15 minutes

    1 hour   half hour   15 minutes

How long might each activity take? Circle the correct answer.

   washing
your hands

2 minutes   2 hours

   frosting
a cake

2 minutes   half hour

Circle the activity that takes longer to do.

Problem solving with time

Figure out the answer to each problem.

Sal starts school in 15 minutes.
At what time does Sal start school?

9 : 15

Josie feeds her cat at 10.20.
How much time will pass before she feeds her cat?

[ ] minutes

You have 30 minutes to finish reading.
At what time must you finish?

[ ] : [ ]

Mary will go to bed in 6 hours.
At what time will Mary go to bed?

[ ] : [ ]

Matt must do three small jobs. Each job will take about 15 minutes.
Then Matt wants to meet Uncle Fred for lunch at 12.00. It is a
1 minute bike ride to Uncle Fred's. Matt starts his jobs at 11.00.
Will Matt get to lunch by 12.00? Circle "yes" or "no".

Yes   No

Symmetry

Draw a line of symmetry on each picture.

Draw lines of symmetry on these shapes.

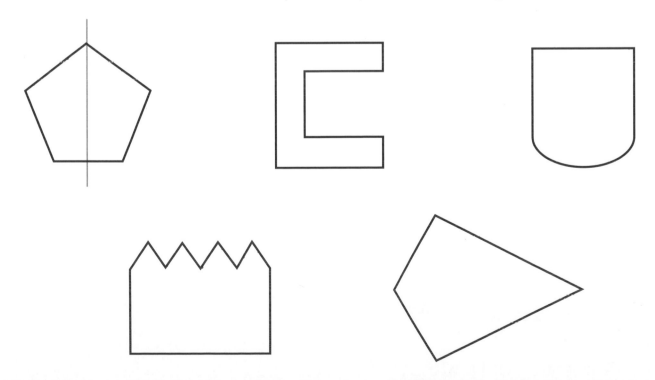

3D shapes

Write the name of the shape and count the corners.

cuboid   cylinder   sphere   cube   square-based pyramid

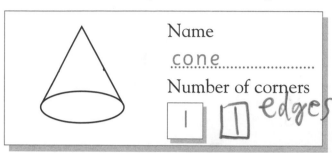

Name cone

Number of corners

| 1 | 1 edges |

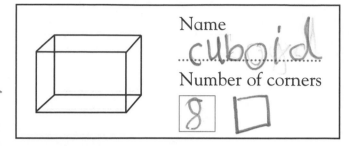

Name cuboid

Number of corners

| 8 | ☐ |

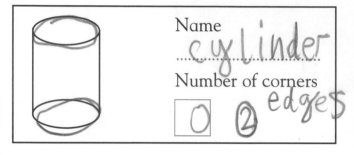

Name cylinder

Number of corners

| 0 | ② edges |

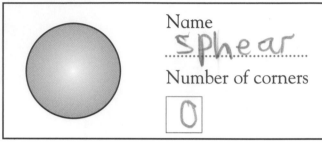

Name sphear

Number of corners

| 0 |

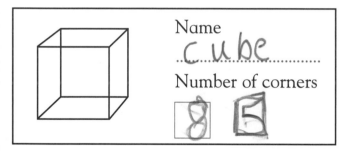

Name cube

Number of corners

| 8 | 5 |

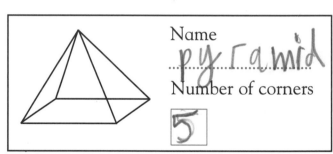

Name pyramid

Number of corners

| 5 |

Thinking about faces

shapes with curved faces   shapes with flat faces

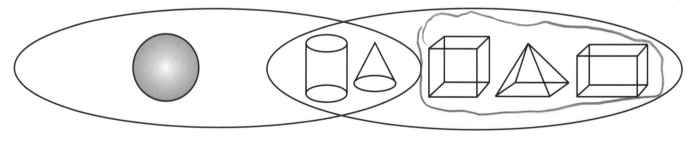

Which shapes have no curved faces? ....

Which shape has no flat faces? ....

Why are the cone and the cylinder in the middle? ....

....

Which shapes have flat faces? ....

28

Shapes and places

Look at the shapes and answer the questions.

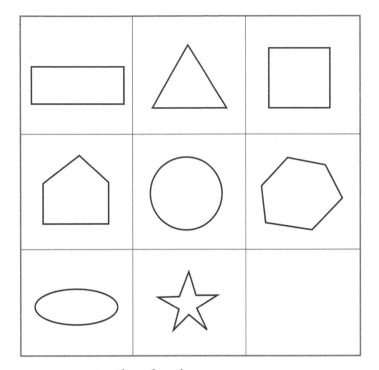

circle

hexagon

oval

pentagon

rectangle

square

star

triangle

Which shape is ...

underneath the circle? ....

on the **left** of the triangle? ....

above the hexagon? ....

below the pentagon? ....

between the rectangle and the oval? ....

diagonally above the empty space? ....

by the side of the oval? ....

on top of the oval? ....

between the triangle and the star? ....

on the **right-hand end** of the top row? ....

in the **centre** of the grid? ....

in the **top left-hand corner**? ....

Tables and grids

Water animals

	Has 4 legs	Eats insects	Has a furry coat	Lays eggs
frog	✓	✓	✗	✓
newt	✓	✓	✗	✓
otter	✓	✗	✓	✗

Use the grid to answer the questions.

What does the ....insects............... frog eat?

Who lays eggs? ....

Who has a furry coat? ....

Does the otter .... eat insects?

Who has a furry coat and does not lay eggs? ....

School friends

	Age	Hobby	Pet	Favourite colour
Dean	7	computers	rat	black
Zoë	6	reading	rabbit	purple
Taif	7	judo	cat	orange
Maddie	8	computers	parrot	green

Use the grid to answer the questions.

Whose favourite colour is black? ....Dean's..........

Who is the eldest? ....

Who has judo for a hobby? ....

What kind of pet has Zoë got? ....

Who likes computers and has a parrot? ....

Who is seven and does not have a rat? ....

Bar charts

Look at the bar chart and then answer the question.

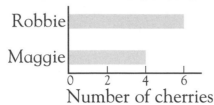

How many cherries does Robbie have?

6

Look at the bar chart and then answer the questions.

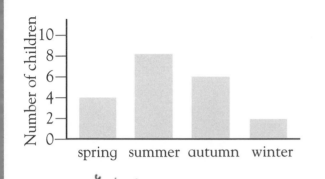

This chart shows the favourite seasons of a group of children.

How many children said which season they liked best?

How many children liked autumn best?

Which season did 4 children like? ....

How many more children liked autumn than winter?

Which was the favourite season? ....

Look at the bar chart and then answer the questions.

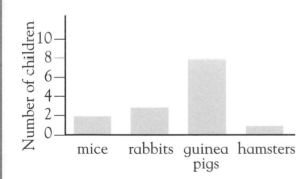

This chart shows the favourite pets of a group of children.

How many children were asked about which pets they liked?

Which pet did 8 children like?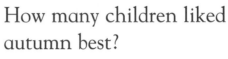

How many children liked rabbits?

How many children liked hamsters?

How many more children liked rabbits than liked hamsters?

Location

The child makes a quarter turn clockwise. What does she see?

.......owl.......

Write what the child will see each time she or he makes the turns.

A quarter turn anti-clockwise.

....

A half turn clockwise.

....

A quarter turn clockwise.

....

A half turn anti-clockwise.

....

A quarter turn anti-clockwise.

....

A half turn clockwise.

....

Answer Section with Parents' Notes
Key Stage 1
Ages 6–7
Advanced

This 8-page section provides answers to all the activities in this book. This will enable you to mark your children's work or can be used by them if they prefer to do their own marking.

The notes for each page help explain the common pitfalls and problems and, where appropriate, give indications as to what practice is needed to ensure your children understand where they have gone wrong.

---

2 ⭐ Up to 100

Write the missing numbers on the kites in each row.

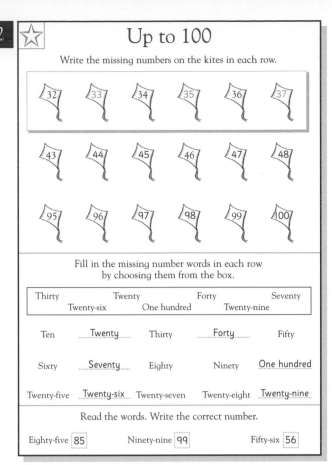

Fill in the missing number words in each row by choosing them from the box.

Thirty	Twenty	Forty	Seventy
Twenty-six	One hundred	Twenty-nine	

Ten	Twenty	Thirty	Forty	Fifty
Sixty	Seventy	Eighty	Ninety	One hundred
Twenty-five	Twenty-six	Twenty-seven	Twenty-eight	Twenty-nine

Read the words. Write the correct number.

Eighty-five 85   Ninety-nine 99   Fifty-six 56

Take children out for a walk and point out house numbers and numbers on signs and hoardings. Ask children to say if the number they can see is greater or less than the one they saw before.

---

3 Changing tens ⭐

Write the number and then the word in each row.

	Number	Word
The value of 4 in 47 is	40	Forty
The value of 8 in 183 is	80	Eighty
The value of 6 in 62 is	60	Sixty
The value of 2 in 126 is	20	Twenty
The value of 5 in 150 is	50	Fifty

Write the answer as a number and as a word in each row.

	Number	Word
If you change 21 to 51, how much value did you add?	30	Thirty
If you change 43 to 83, how much value did you add?	40	Forty
If you change 65 to 35, how much value did you subtract?	30	Thirty

Circle the numbers in which the 2 has a value of 20.

82   (28)   (125)

Ask children to identify the number of tens in a number. Make sure they understand that writing tens in numeric form (10s) will include a 0, yet the word form will not include the word zero.

---

4 ⭐ Fact families

Complete the facts for each family.

3 + 5 = 8	5 + 3 = 8	8 – 3 = 5	8 – 5 = 3
2 + 7 = 9	7 + 2 = 9	9 – 2 = 7	9 – 7 = 2
3 + 4 = 7	4 + 3 = 7	7 – 3 = 4	7 – 4 = 3
4 + 5 = 9	5 + 4 = 9	9 – 4 = 5	9 – 5 = 4
1 + 6 = 7	6 + 1 = 7	7 – 1 = 6	7 – 6 = 1
6 + 4 = 10	4 + 6 = 10	10 – 4 = 6	10 – 6 = 4
5 + 2 = 7	2 + 5 = 7	7 – 5 = 2	7 – 2 = 5
1 + 8 = 9	8 + 1 = 9	9 – 8 = 1	9 – 1 = 8
7 + 3 = 10	3 + 7 = 10	10 – 7 = 3	10 – 3 = 7

Write the facts for the fact family 3, 6, and 9.

6 + 3 = 9   9 – 6 = 3
3 + 6 = 9   9 – 3 = 6

Divide ten beans into two groups, and invite children to write the addition sentence for the two groups of beans. Repeat, varying the group sizes. Then put all the beans together and remove between one and nine beans, asking the child to write the subtraction sentence.

Quick adding

Write the answers.

$$7 + 2 = \boxed{9}$$ $$9 + 0 = \boxed{9}$$ $$2 + 3 = \boxed{5}$$ $$5 + 4 = \boxed{9}$$ $$4 + 6 = \boxed{10}$$

$$1 + 2 = \boxed{3}$$ $$10 + 0 = \boxed{10}$$ $$4 + 4 = \boxed{8}$$ $$5 + 3 = \boxed{8}$$ $$4 + 2 = \boxed{6}$$

$$5 + 2 = \boxed{7}$$ $$6 + 3 = \boxed{9}$$ $$3 + 3 = \boxed{6}$$ $$5 + 0 = \boxed{5}$$ $$9 + 1 = \boxed{10}$$

Write the missing number.

$$\boxed{4} + 6 = 10 \qquad 2 + \boxed{6} = 8 \qquad 6 + \boxed{3} = 9$$

$$\boxed{7} + 1 = 8 \qquad \boxed{2} + 5 = 7 \qquad 3 + \boxed{4} = 7$$

$$0 + \boxed{10} = 10 \qquad 4 + \boxed{2} = 6 \qquad \boxed{4} + 4 = 8$$

Write the number sentence to match the pictures.

$$\boxed{2} + \boxed{8} = \boxed{10}$$

$$\boxed{3} + \boxed{5} = \boxed{8}$$

Practice quick addition facts regularly with your child. Children should also be encouraged to use mental arithmetic for the basic addition facts.

☆ Adding two-digit numbers

Use the number lines to answer the equations in each row.

13 14 15 16 17 18 19 20 21 22 23 24 25 26 27 28 29 30 31 32

$$13 + 12 = \boxed{25}$$ $$14 + 13 = \boxed{27}$$ $$21 + 11 = \boxed{32}$$ $$17 + 10 = \boxed{27}$$ $$11 + 21 = \boxed{32}$$

20 21 22 23 24 25 26 27 28 29 30 31 32 33 34 35 36

$$24 + 12 = \boxed{36}$$ $$21 + 11 = \boxed{32}$$ $$23 + 10 = \boxed{33}$$ $$25 + 10 = \boxed{35}$$ $$20 + 13 = \boxed{33}$$

28 29 30 31 32 33 34 35 36 37 38 39 40 41 42

$$30 + 12 = \boxed{42}$$ $$28 + 10 = \boxed{38}$$ $$31 + 11 = \boxed{42}$$ $$30 + 10 = \boxed{40}$$ $$29 + 10 = \boxed{39}$$

Use the counting blocks to solve the equations.

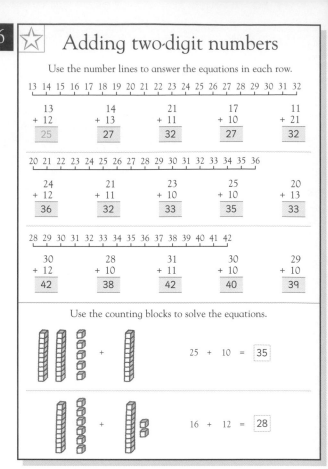

$$25 + 10 = \boxed{35}$$

$$16 + 12 = \boxed{28}$$

Draw a number line on a piece of paper. Say an addition sentence, and let children move along the line to find the sum. For each addition sentence, make sure that the child understands where to start on the number line.

Adding numbers vertically

Add the ones, then add the tens in each equation. Write the answer.

Add the ones, Tens Ones	then the tens. Tens Ones	Regroup and add.
7 4 + 1 2 8 **6**	7 4 + 1 2 **8** 6	¹ 6 2 + 1 9 8 1

$$63 + 31 = \boxed{94}$$ $$45 + 20 = \boxed{65}$$ $$14 + 14 = \boxed{28}$$ $$35 + 31 = \boxed{66}$$ $$54 + 22 = \boxed{76}$$

$$75 + 23 = \boxed{98}$$ $$18 + 20 = \boxed{38}$$ $$14 + 82 = \boxed{96}$$ $$74 + 11 = \boxed{85}$$ $$50 + 32 = \boxed{82}$$

Add the ones, and regroup your answer as tens and ones. Then add the tens to solve each equation.

$$\overset{1}{5}3 + 38 = \boxed{91}$$ $$\overset{1}{4}8 + 32 = \boxed{80}$$ $$\overset{1}{1}6 + 14 = \boxed{30}$$ $$\overset{1}{6}2 + 19 = \boxed{81}$$ $$\overset{1}{4}4 + 47 = \boxed{91}$$

$$\overset{1}{5}5 + 18 = \boxed{73}$$ $$\overset{1}{3}9 + 33 = \boxed{72}$$ $$\overset{1}{2}8 + 14 = \boxed{42}$$ $$\overset{1}{4}6 + 29 = \boxed{75}$$ $$\overset{1}{1}7 + 46 = \boxed{63}$$

Write the answer to each equation. Shade the shapes where the answer is 79.

37 + 42 = 79	52 + 27 = 79	33 + 59 = 92	61 + 18 = 79	43 + 15 = 58	24 + 55 = 79

Show children how to draw a vertical line separating the tens and ones columns, when adding two-digit numbers vertically. Explain that if adding the ones results in ten or more ones, they need to regroup those ones before adding the tens.

☆ Problem solving (addition)

Read each story. Then write the equation and solve the problem.

Mr. Lopez sells apples. He has 4 baskets of 10 apples, and another 8 loose apples. How many apples does he have in his store?

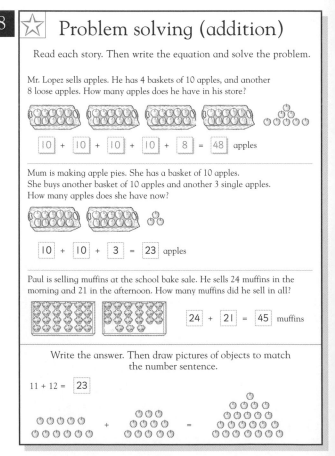

$$\boxed{10} + \boxed{10} + \boxed{10} + \boxed{10} + \boxed{8} = \boxed{48} \text{ apples}$$

Mum is making apple pies. She has a basket of 10 apples. She buys another basket of 10 apples and another 3 single apples. How many apples does she have now?

$$\boxed{10} + \boxed{10} + \boxed{3} = \boxed{23} \text{ apples}$$

Paul is selling muffins at the school bake sale. He sells 24 muffins in the morning and 21 in the afternoon. How many muffins did he sell in all?

$$\boxed{24} + \boxed{21} = \boxed{45} \text{ muffins}$$

Write the answer. Then draw pictures of objects to match the number sentence.

$$11 + 12 = \boxed{23}$$

Provide children with different types of objects, such as a collection of small plastic toys or some crayons or some wooden bricks. Then ask the children to use the various groups of objects to create and solve their own word problems involving addition.

Subtraction action

Write the answers to these subtraction problems.

10	9	7	10	8
− 7	− 3	− 5	− 2	− 4
3	6	2	8	4

9	5	6	9	4
− 6	− 3	− 1	− 4	− 4
3	2	5	5	0

3	7	6	10	2
− 1	− 2	− 3	− 5	− 2
2	5	3	5	0

Fill in the missing number in each subtraction problem.

8 − 6 = 2   8 − 7 = 1   4 − 2 = 2

10 − 6 = 4   9 − 7 = 2   10 − 8 = 2

Complete the number sentences. Shade in the animal that has a number sentence with an answer less than 5.

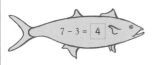
7 − 3 = 4

10 − 4 = 6

Make time to practise quick subtraction facts regularly with your child. As with basic addition facts, encourage children to use mental arithmetic when working with basic subtraction facts.

Find the difference

Count backward on the number lines to solve the equations in each row.

24 25 26 27 28 29 30 31 32 33 34 35 36 37 38 39 40 41 42

42	35	39	37	41
− 11	− 10	− 15	− 11	− 10
31	25	24	26	31

65 66 67 68 69 70 71 72 73 74 75 76 77 78 79 80 81 82 83 84 85

80	85	75	76	83
− 10	− 13	− 10	− 11	− 12
70	72	65	65	71

50 51 52 53 54 55 56 57 58 59 60 61 62 63 64 65 66 67 68 69 70

70	62	65	65	64
− 20	− 12	− 10	− 11	− 12
50	50	55	54	52

Draw dots in the boxes to show 22 − 12 = 10.

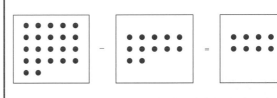

For practice, draw your own number line, place a plastic counter at its end, and roll a dice. Ask your child to move the counter back along the line by the number on the rolled dice. Also ask your child to write the corresponding subtraction sentence.

What's the difference?

Find the difference in each subtraction problem.

Subtract the ones,	then the tens.	Regroup and subtract.
Tens Ones	Tens Ones	4 13
7 4	7 4	5̶ 3̶
− 1 2	− 1 2	− 1 4
6 2	6 2	3 9

48	45	88	54	86
− 30	− 15	− 77	− 33	− 54
18	30	11	21	32

89	34	52	74	96
− 54	− 13	− 31	− 23	− 35
35	21	21	51	61

Find the difference by regrouping. Add 10 more to the ones. Make the tens less by 1. Subtract the ones and then the tens.

6 12	7 17	4 13	5 15	7 14
7̶ 2̶	8̶ 7̶	5̶ 3̶	6̶ 5̶	8̶ 4̶
− 5 4	− 2 9	− 2 6	− 4 7	− 6 7
18	58	27	18	17

4 15	2 16	6 15	3 14	5 15
5̶ 5̶	3̶ 6̶	7̶ 5̶	4̶ 4̶	6̶ 5̶
− 1 6	− 1 7	− 4 6	− 2 7	− 4 9
39	19	29	17	16

Draw balloons to show this subtraction sentence. Then write the answer.

17 − 12 = 5

Help children draw a line separating the tens and ones columns when subtracting two-digit numbers vertically. Remind children that if there are fewer ones in the top number than in the bottom number, they must regroup one ten as ten ones first.

Problem solving (subtraction)

Read each story. Solve the problem.

Amy has 65 pages to read for homework. She has already read 31 pages. How many pages does she have left to read?

65 − 31 = 34 pages

It is 32 miles to the airport. Mr. Miller has already driven 21 miles. How many more miles does Mr. Miller need to drive to get to the airport?

32 − 21 = 11 miles

Juan has a list of 21 items to buy at the store. He has already found 11 of the items. How many more items must he find?

21 − 11 = 10 items

Find these words hidden in the puzzle. Go across or down.

takeaway	difference
subtract	minus
equal	

C	Y	M	I	O	S	T	J	H	S
T	W	V	F	P	U	L	K	Z	T
U	A	O	E	G	B	D	X	S	A
M	M	A	S	V	T	Y	I	U	K
D	I	F	F	E	R	E	N	C	E
R	N	E	S	Q	A	D	G	O	A
K	U	L	Q	U	C	X	C	B	W
T	S	I	O	A	T	K	Q	D	A
E	R	P	K	L	I	V	F	J	Y
W	U	H	S	Y	E	P	L	A	X

First ask your child to solve each subtraction word problem. Then ask him or her to give an explanation of how he or she worked out the answers.

Bigger or smaller?

Draw the crocodiles.
They always eat the bigger numbers!

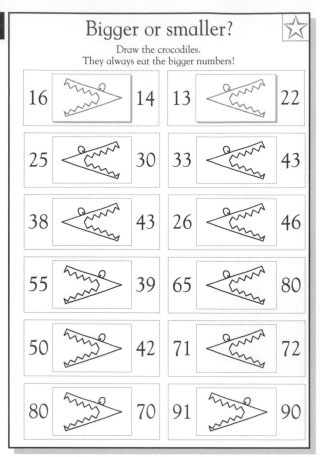

It is important to check that your child understands the words "bigger" and "smaller" as being different to "big" and "small". A child may see numbers such as 71 and 90 as being very big, but they are still smaller than the numbers they are being compared to.

Ordering

Find the totals.

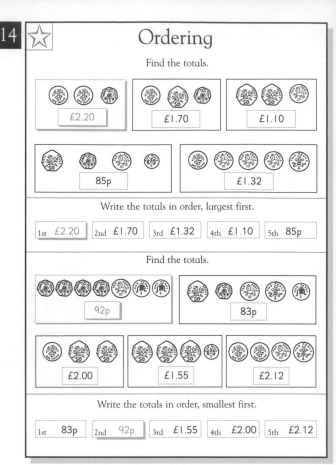

This page revises the operations of addition. No "p" sign should be used with the "£". For example, it should be £1.50 and not £1.50p. Talk about strategies for adding, such as whether it helps to add the larger or smaller value coins first.

Shopping

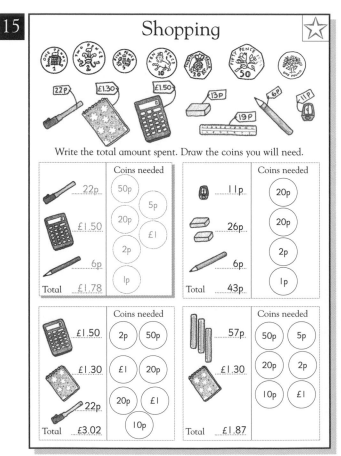

If children draw lower value coins to make up the correct amount, praise them but explain the need to use fewer coins. They must write the unit (p or £) each time. Remember that there is no "p" needed if a "£" has already been used.

2x table

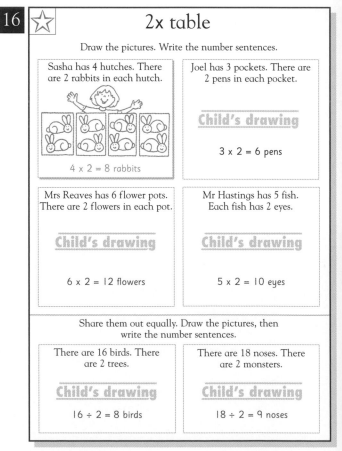

As an additional activity, ask your child to make up simple stories of their own based on the 2 times table. He or she should also try making a drawing as well as writing out the story and the number sentence.

10x table

Find the right label for each balloon.
Only use the labels you really need.

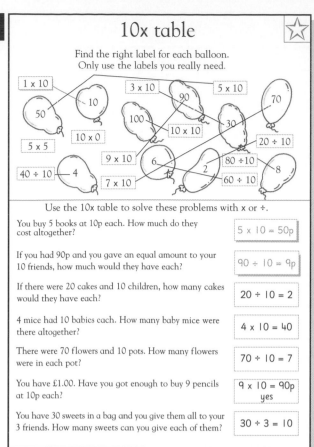

Use the 10x table to solve these problems with x or ÷.

You buy 5 books at 10p each. How much do they cost altogether?

$5 \times 10 = 50p$

If you had 90p and you gave an equal amount to your 10 friends, how much would they have each?

$90 \div 10 = 9p$

If there were 20 cakes and 10 children, how many cakes would they have each?

$20 \div 10 = 2$

4 mice had 10 babies each. How many baby mice were there altogether?

$4 \times 10 = 40$

There were 70 flowers and 10 pots. How many flowers were in each pot?

$70 \div 10 = 7$

You have £1.00. Have you got enough to buy 9 pencils at 10p each?

$9 \times 10 = 90p$
yes

You have 30 sweets in a bag and you give them all to your 3 friends. How many sweets can you give each of them?

$30 \div 3 = 10$

Two labels not linked to any balloon are included to help children choose answers. They must also decide whether to multiply or divide to get the correct answer to the problems.

5x table

Find the right pot for each flower. Not all pots will have a flower.

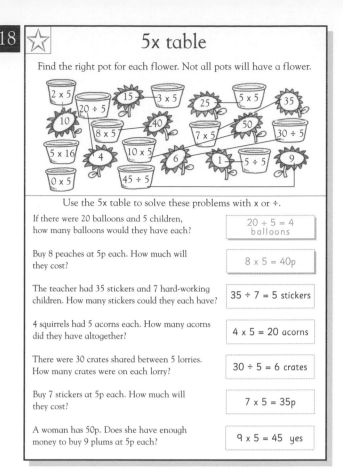

Use the 5x table to solve these problems with x or ÷.

If there were 20 balloons and 5 children, how many balloons would they have each?

$20 \div 5 = 4$
balloons

Buy 8 peaches at 5p each. How much will they cost?

$8 \times 5 = 40p$

The teacher had 35 stickers and 7 hard-working children. How many stickers could they each have?

$35 \div 7 = 5$ stickers

4 squirrels had 5 acorns each. How many acorns did they have altogether?

$4 \times 5 = 20$ acorns

There were 30 crates shared between 5 lorries. How many crates were on each lorry?

$30 \div 5 = 6$ crates

Buy 7 stickers at 5p each. How much will they cost?

$7 \times 5 = 35p$

A woman has 50p. Does she have enough money to buy 9 plums at 5p each?

$9 \times 5 = 45$ yes

The notes for page 17 are also relevant here. If children do not readily see that flower 1 links to 5 ÷ 5, it may help to say in words, "If 5 (things) are shared between 5 (people), how many would each get?".

Rectangular arrays

Count the rows and columns. Then write the multiplication sentence.

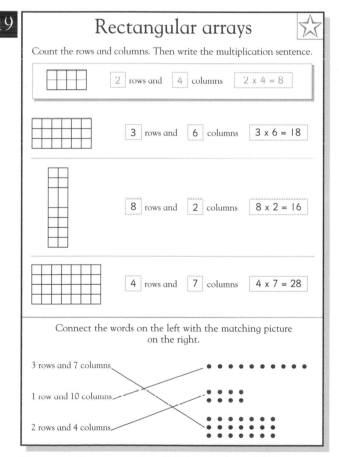

2 rows and 4 columns $2 \times 4 = 8$

3 rows and 6 columns $3 \times 6 = 18$

8 rows and 2 columns $8 \times 2 = 16$

4 rows and 7 columns $4 \times 7 = 28$

Connect the words on the left with the matching picture on the right.

3 rows and 7 columns

1 row and 10 columns

2 rows and 4 columns

Rectangular arrays let children see multiplication in a different way. For consistency, read arrays based on the number of rows, then the number of columns. An array of four columns and three rows is a 3 x 4 rectangular array.

Real-life problems

Look at the picture. Answer the questions.

What time is it? 4:30

Today is Friday. What day was it yesterday? Thursday

How many cakes can each person have? two

If half of the apples were eaten, how many would be left? three

If each person had 2 drinks, how many drinks would there be altogether? eight

How many more sandwiches are there than apples? four

If 13 sweets were eaten, how many would be left? seven

Each parcel contains 2 presents. How many presents are there altogether? six

What shape are the sandwiches? triangle

Is there an odd or an even number of chairs? even

Children will first have to decide what each question is asking them to do and then establish their own way of calculating the answer. For example, do they realise that the fifth question is asking for 4 x 2?

Estimating mass

Circle the animal that is probably heavier in each pair.

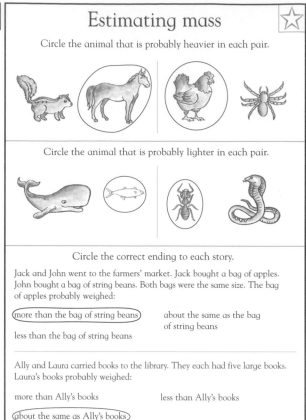

Circle the animal that is probably lighter in each pair.

Circle the correct ending to each story.

Jack and John went to the farmers' market. Jack bought a bag of apples. John bought a bag of string beans. Both bags were the same size. The bag of apples probably weighed:

(more than the bag of string beans)   about the same as the bag of string beans

less than the bag of string beans

Ally and Laura carried books to the library. They each had five large books. Laura's books probably weighed:

more than Ally's books   less than Ally's books

(about the same as Ally's books)

Try and provide some extra word problems that will help your child practise estimation. Explain that estimation is not the same as guessing. Instead, it is a way to predict an amount based on the information that you have.

Measuring lengths

How many centimetres long are these objects?

10 cm long

12 cm long

8 cm long

9 cm long

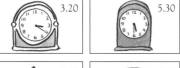
6 cm long

Encourage your child to use rulers to measure the lengths of various objects around your house or neighbourhood. Make sure that the unit of measurement, such as centimetres (cm) or metres (m), is included when recording measurements.

Problem solving (lengths)

Read each story. Then add or subtract the lengths to solve the problems.

Tom and Jason measured the flowers they found. Tom's flower measured 25 cm while Jason's was 20 cm long. What was the difference in the lengths of the flowers?

25 cm – 20 cm = 5 cm

Jess bought a piece of ribbon that was 27 cm long. Mary bought one that was 15 cm long. How long were the two pieces altogether?

27 cm + 15 cm = 42 cm

Maria's coloured pencil was 22 cm long. Juan's coloured pencil was 15 cm long. How much longer was Maria's pencil than Juan's?

22 cm – 15 cm = 7 cm

Maya watched an ant crawl 7 cm Then the ant crawled 17 cm more. How many centimetres did the ant crawl altogether?

7 cm + 17 cm = 24 cm

Linda's drawing paper was 30 cm long. Sue's paper was 25 cm long. How much longer was Linda's paper than Sue's?

30 cm – 25 cm = 5 cm

Anita has a piece of string that is 24 cm long.
Can she make two equal pieces from this piece of string?   (Yes)   No

How long would each piece be?   12 cm

Encourage children to read problem-solving questions carefully, to first determine exactly what the question is asking. Then they should determine which operation they should use to reach the correct answer.

Telling the time

Draw the hands on the clock to show twenty past 5.

Draw the hands on each clock to show the time.

3.20   5.30   8.35

7.45   9.25   11.15

Write the time shown on each clock.

12.15   1.40   12.05

2.10   6.30   8.05

At this stage, children should know how to tell the time to the nearest 5 minutes and be able to draw it on a clock face. The last section offers further practice in reading the time shown on an analogue clock.

Differences between times

Look at the time on the first clock in each row. Then look at the time on the second clock. What is the difference in time between the clocks? Circle the correct answer.

1 hour   half hour   (15 minutes)

1 hour   half hour   15 minutes

(1 hour)   half hour   15 minutes

How long might each activity take? Circle the correct answer.

washing your hands
(2 minutes)   2 hours

frosting a cake
2 minutes   (half hour)

Circle the activity that takes longer to do.

Let children practise using a clock to identify a starting time before they carry out a simple task, such as fastening a shoe. Then ask them to check the time when they finish. Encourage them to work out how much time has passed.

Problem solving with time

Figure out the answer to each problem.

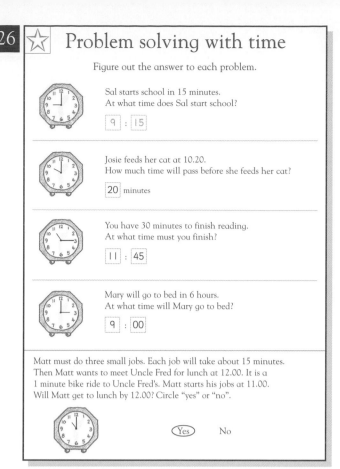

Sal starts school in 15 minutes.
At what time does Sal start school?
[9] : [15]

Josie feeds her cat at 10.20.
How much time will pass before she feeds her cat?
[20] minutes

You have 30 minutes to finish reading.
At what time must you finish?
[11] : [45]

Mary will go to bed in 6 hours.
At what time will Mary go to bed?
[9] : [00]

Matt must do three small jobs. Each job will take about 15 minutes. Then Matt wants to meet Uncle Fred for lunch at 12.00. It is a 1 minute bike ride to Uncle Fred's. Matt starts his jobs at 11.00. Will Matt get to lunch by 12.00? Circle "yes" or "no".

(Yes)   No

Think up more problem-solving time questions to ask your child. If you have a toy clock, try using it to determine the answers. Make sure that your child uses the correct terms (minutes or hours) when answering.

Symmetry

Draw a line of symmetry on each picture.

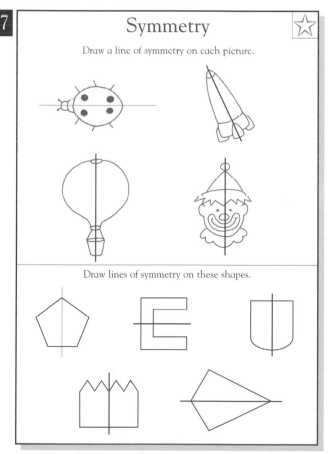

Draw lines of symmetry on these shapes.

Ask your child to explain what a line of symmetry is. Test if he or she can relate this to knowing that halves of anything have to be exactly the same. If your child finds this activity difficult, they could draw shapes on paper and fold them in half to find the line of symmetry.

3D shapes

Write the name of the shape and count the corners.

cuboid   cylinder   sphere   cube   square-based pyramid

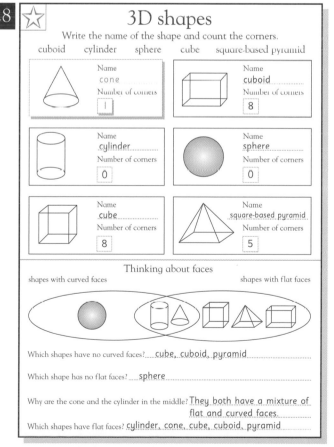

Name: cone
Number of corners: 1

Name: cuboid
Number of corners: 8

Name: cylinder
Number of corners: 0

Name: sphere
Number of corners: 0

Name: cube
Number of corners: 8

Name: square-based pyramid
Number of corners: 5

Thinking about faces

shapes with curved faces   shapes with flat faces

Which shapes have no curved faces? cube, cuboid, pyramid

Which shape has no flat faces? sphere

Why are the cone and the cylinder in the middle? They both have a mixture of flat and curved faces.

Which shapes have flat faces? cylinder, cone, cube, cuboid, pyramid

If your child finds it difficult to count corners or to identify faces from the diagrams, let him or her find real examples of the shapes in the kitchen or in their toy box. They could then begin to count the faces. Can your child see that a sphere only has one face?

Shapes and places

Look at the shapes and answer the questions.

circle
hexagon
oval
pentagon
rectangle
square
star
triangle

Which shape is ...

underneath the circle? .... star

on the **left** of the triangle? .... rectangle

above the hexagon? .... square

below the pentagon? .... oval

between the rectangle and the oval? .... pentagon

diagonally above the empty space? .... circle

by the side of the oval? .... star

on top of the oval? .... pentagon

between the triangle and the star? .... circle

on the **right-hand end** of the top row? .... square

in the **centre** of the grid? .... circle

in the **top left-hand corner**? .... rectangle

This page helps children to understand positional vocabulary. They may need help with the questions. It is not designed to test the spellings, so shapes are listed for reference.

Tables and grids

Water animals

	Has 4 legs	Eats insects	Has a furry coat	Lays eggs
frog	✓	✓	✗	✓
newt	✓	✓	✗	✓
otter	✓	✗	✓	✗

Use the grid to answer the questions.

What does the frog eat? .... insects

Who lays eggs? .... frog, newt

Who has a furry coat? .... otter

Does the otter eat insects? .... no

Who has a furry coat and does not lay eggs? .... otter

School friends

	Age	Hobby	Pet	Favourite colour
Dean	7	computers	rat	black
Zoë	6	reading	rabbit	purple
Taif	7	judo	cat	orange
Maddie	8	computers	parrot	green

Use the grid to answer the questions.

Whose favourite colour is black? .... Dean's

Who is the eldest? .... Maddie

Who has judo for a hobby? .... Taif

What kind of pet has Zoë got? .... rabbit

Who likes computers and has a parrot? .... Maddie

Who is seven and does not have a rat? .... Taif

If your child finds it difficult to focus on the right box, they can use two pencils or two fingers, and slide them along the row and down the column. Where they "bump" is the right box. Techniques for reading simple grids will help them with complex ones later.

Bar charts

Look at the bar chart and then answer the question.

Robbie
Maggie

0 2 4 6
Number of cherries

How many cherries does Robbie have? 6

Look at the bar chart and then answer the questions.

Number of children: 10 8 6 4 2 0
spring summer autumn winter

This chart shows the favourite seasons of a group of children.

How many children said which season they liked best? 20

How many children liked autumn best? 6

Which season did 4 children like? spring

How many more children liked autumn than winter? 4

Which was the favourite season? summer

Look at the bar chart and then answer the questions.

Number of children: 10 8 6 4 2 0
mice rabbits guinea pigs hamsters

This chart shows the favourite pets of a group of children.

How many children were asked about which pets they liked? 14

Which pet did 8 children like? guinea pigs

How many children liked rabbits? 3

How many children liked hamsters? 1

How many more children liked rabbits than liked hamsters? 2

Children must realise that the units on the side of the chart are in twos, not ones. This is especially important in the second half, where some readings fall between the unit sections, and children will need to recognise that these are appropriate odd numbers.

Location

The child makes a quarter turn clockwise. What does she see?

.... owl

Write what the child will see each time she or he makes the turns.

A quarter turn anti-clockwise. .... cow

A half turn clockwise. .... pig

A quarter turn clockwise. .... snake

A half turn anti-clockwise. .... hat

A quarter turn anti-clockwise. .... keys

A half turn clockwise. .... pear

Children need to understand that a half turn means 180° and it does not matter if is clockwise or anti-clockwise. With a quarter turn, it is important to get the direction correct. Children may want to physically move the book around to find the answer.